Release the Power of the BLOOD COVENANT

By Marilyn Hickey

P.O. Box 17340 • Denver, Colorado 80217

Release the Power of the Blood Covenant

Copyright © 1994 by Marilyn Hickey
Ministries
P.O. Box 17340
Denver, Colorado 80217
All Rights Reserved
ISBN 1-56441-056-6

All scriptures are quoted from the
King James Version of the Bible
unless otherwise indicated.

Printed in the United States of America

CONTENTS

Chapter One
    Life Is in the Blood 5

Chapter Two
    His Promises Are True 27

Chapter Three
    Old Testament Covenants 35

Chapter Four
    Forever and Ever 53

Chapter Five
    Your Spiritual Blood Line 59

Chapter Six
    Open-heart Surgery 75

Chapter Seven
    The Blood and the Word 81

Chapter One
Life Is in the Blood

The Bible is a book full of life; therefore, it is a book full of blood. From Genesis to Revelation, we see the importance of the blood of life.

As a child of God, every Christian needs to know what "covenant relationship" means to him or her; and more importantly, what is the significance of the **blood covenant**. Unfortunately, while many Christians understand that they are in covenant relationship with God, they have no knowledge of the covenant rights and promises that are theirs because of the blood of Jesus. Consequently, they live far below their heavenly Father's means.

These kinds of Christians are like the man who scrimped and saved to buy a ticket to America. After he bought his ticket, he only had enough money left to buy a little bread and cheese to eat on the trip. During the long voyage, he gazed longingly into the ship's dining room every day, dreaming of feasts fit for a king. Finally the trip came to an end, and as he was disembarking, one of the ship's crew asked him, "Did we offend you? You didn't eat in the dining room with the rest of the passengers."

"No," he replied. "I just didn't have enough money to pay for the meals."

"Oh, I'm so sorry," said the ship's officer. "Didn't you know that your meals were included in the price of your ticket?"

How sad it is to think that so many Christians have entered into covenant with their loving heavenly Father, but—like this poor man—have no idea of the provisions He has made for them through His eternal blood covenant. Or worse, they think they have to pay for all the benefits that come with the New Covenant or prove themselves worthy enough of the new life Jesus bought for them. They just don't understand—Jesus' blood paid the price for their eternal life. So let's see how this blood covenant works!

What Is a Covenant?

Of all the agreements, contracts, treaties, or pacts ever devised by mankind, perhaps none is more binding upon the parties involved than a *blood covenant*. It is so binding that one of the first recorded covenants between God and man has endured from the time of Adam until the present and extends even into eternity.

Since the time of Adam, covenants have been a way of life in almost every culture of the world. History is full of accounts of different kinds of covenants, and the knowledge of many of these

Life Is in the Blood

covenants has been passed down from one generation to another. For example, *threshold covenants* were made by offering sacrifices at the threshold, thereby honoring guests, warding off evil spirits, or bringing good luck to the household. *Wedding covenants* used rings, bracelets, or armlets to signify betrothal or marriage. *Friendship covenants*, widely practiced throughout the world, were a pledge of friendship or loyalty. No matter the tribe or nation, there is one common thread—virtually every ancient covenant included the shedding of blood in some form or another.

In today's world, the idea of bloodshed is considered barbaric or heathenish at the very least—even though many of the tribes and nations in some underdeveloped countries still incorporate the practice of blood covenants into their daily lives. Today, the definition of a *covenant* has been expanded to mean, "an agreement, promise, pledge, association, or meeting (usually formal) between two or more persons or parties who agree to do or not do something specific." Here in the United States, lawyers, judges, government officials, and witnesses are usually involved to make the covenant binding.

To the human race, though, the shedding of blood in a covenant is the only way to ensure a new beginning and eternal life. You see, even in prehistoric times, people believed that blood could bring life back to the dead. The belief in vampires and ghouls seems to have been an outgrowth of this thought. This was a warped perception of the truth that God has tried to get across to people since the time of Adam and Eve: death was a result of sin and there could be no new life without the remission of sin. So God developed a plan to restore life to sinners:

And almost all things are by the law purged with blood; and without shedding of blood is no remission (Hebrews 9:22).

Without the shedding of blood there is no remission of sin, no new beginnings, no eternal life. In the Old Testament, the blood of animals was substituted for men; their blood was shed upon the altars in ceremonies, offerings, sacrifices, and feasts to compensate for the sins of man. During the thousands of years between the time the law was given and the time it was fulfilled in Jesus Christ, millions of animals had to be slain just to keep up with the sins of the people of Israel. Sacrifices and offerings were a daily occurrence in the Tabernacle and later in the Temple. Blood was constantly flowing down the altars. But with the Crucifixion and death of Jesus, sacrifices and offerings were rendered null and void. When God sent Jesus to die on the Cross, Jesus "cut" the final covenant between God and man, pouring out His blood to make atonement for the sins of

Life Is in the Blood

the world:

For God so loved the world, that he gave his only begotten Son, that whosoever believeth in him should not perish, but have everlasting life (John 3:16).

Jesus became the ultimate sacrifice; His was the only blood acceptable to the Father to give new life to a sinful people and restore them to fellowship with the Father once and for all.

Even before you were born, God loved you so much that He sacrificed His only Son for YOU. The blood that Jesus shed for you initiated the New Covenant even before your parents and grandparents were born. Even if you were the only person to have ever been born, God still would have sent Jesus to die for you. The blood covenant would have been established just for your protection and security, the Cross would have been built to serve as an altar of atonement for your sins, and Jesus' blood would have been shed to give you eternal life. To sum it up, the mediator—a perfect mediator would be one who fully understands both parties involved and could represent both parties equally—of the New Covenant is Jesus Christ (see I Timothy 2:5). The power of the New Covenant is the blood. And the reason for the New Covenant is YOU.

The Sacredness of the Blood

From Genesis to Revelation, the Bible is about

blood. God tells us not to eat blood (Leviticus 17:12). Numbers 35:33 tells us that blood pollutes the land on which it is spilt because it cannot be cleansed except by the blood of the person who spilled it. Even if a hunter killed an animal for food, he was to pour out its blood and cover it with dust (see Leviticus 17:13). And if a man killed another man, the penalty was death.

But most importantly, God considers blood sacred because "... *the life of the flesh is in the blood:* ... " (Leviticus 17:11). The blood is alive and brings life to every cell in your body. The life-giving substance in blood constantly supplies your body with strength. In fact, we would all be spiritually dead in trespasses and sin if it were not for the blood of Christ.

The blood is so sacred to God that it even has the power to communicate with Him. After Adam and Eve were cast out of Eden, they passed on the importance of the blood to their children; Cain and Abel knew God required the shedding of blood as an atonement for sins.

One day when Cain and Abel made a sacrifice to God, Abel offered the firstlings of his flock but Cain offered the work of his own hands from the fields. God was pleased with Abel's sacrifice, but He did not respect Cain's offering because there was no blood shed; there was no life taken for another. Cain's own provision was not enough to

Life Is in the Blood

satisfy God's requirement for atonement. When God reprimanded Cain, Cain was unwilling to repent and receive God's forgiveness (Genesis 4:7). Instead, he became jealous of Abel and killed him. God then confronted Cain:

And he [God] *said, What hast thou done? the voice of thy brother's blood crieth unto me from the ground* (Genesis 4:10).

God heard the blood! Blood has a voice *but only* if it is the blood of one who is in covenant relationship with God. When other people were murdered, the Bible doesn't say that God heard their blood cry out. But because Abel was God's covenant child, He heard his blood. God will also hear the blood of Christians because we are in covenant relationship with Him. His blood applied to our lives cries, "mercy, mercy"!

In addition, the Bible tells us that **God smells the blood**. After the flood, Noah and his family sacrificed clean animals to God when they came out of the ark:

And Noah builded an altar unto the LORD; and took of every clean beast, and of every clean fowl, and offered burnt offerings on the altar. ***And the LORD smelled a sweet savour;*** . . . (Genesis 8:20,21).

Not only does God smell blood, but it smells good to Him; He considers it a sweet savor. Likewise, when we are under the blood of Jesus, we are a sweet *smelling* savor to God.

In addition to hearing and smelling blood, **God sees it.** When God told Moses to deliver the Hebrews from Egypt, He also warned him that Pharaoh would not "hearken unto him." So God instituted a series of ten plagues to persuade the Egyptians to release His people from bondage.

I think it's interesting that these ten plagues began with blood and ended with blood. God wanted the Egyptians to see that it was only blood that could give them covenant relationship with the one, true God. The Nile was not a god as the Egyptians believed. In fact, the Nile contained the blood of Jewish babies and, no doubt, God heard their blood crying out to Him.

In the first plague, the Nile River was turned into blood. In the tenth plague, God told the Hebrews to kill the passover lamb and apply its blood to their doorposts. When God **saw** the blood on the doorposts, the death angel passed over the Hebrews' homes but killed the first born of every Egyptian family. Why? Because God didn't see any blood on the Egyptian's homes.

Blood is sacred to God because He gave it to make atonement for sin (Leviticus 17:11). Even before Adam and Eve sinned—from before the foundation of the earth—God had prepared a way for us to restore the communion and fellowship with Him that was lost because of Adam and Eve's

Life Is in the Blood

sin. He planned a new beginning for them and for us through the offering of blood.

When God killed an animal to clothe Adam and Eve, He established His plan of salvation. If you remember, God came looking for Adam in the garden to just sit and chat awhile. He enjoyed those times of fellowship He shared with His children. I often get a mental picture of Adam and Eve running up to God in the cool of the evening to tell Him of the wonderful new discoveries they made that day—much like children who come bursting into the house anxious to tell their parents about a tree decked out in beautiful fall colors or the dog down the street who just had puppies!

But this time when God came to talk with them, something was wrong; they didn't come when they were called. When Adam finally responded, he told God they were hiding from Him because they knew they were naked. They could know that only because they had disobeyed Him—they had sinned. With sin came death and separation from God. Man no longer had immediate access to the presence of the Father. Curses came upon man and all his descendants because of sin: sickness, disease, poverty, depression, hate, greed, envy, lust, etc. Sin became an inherited genetic trait handed down from generation to generation.

Let's look at this more closely. When Adam and

Release the Power of the Blood Covenant

Eve realized they were naked, they tried to make a covering for themselves by sewing fig leaves together. God knew fig leaves weren't sufficient to protect them against the elements of the fallen world or to provide a covering for them, let alone make atonement for their sins. So God killed an animal and clothed them with its skins (Genesis 3:21).

It was at this point we first see the method of salvation laid out for us. I call this the "law of first mention" because it refers to the first instance of a pattern, ceremony, or symbolism mentioned in the Bible that later become a law or rule. The "law of first mention" is probably best exemplified in the plan of salvation because we can trace the laws and rules governing salvation from Genesis to Revelation.

The "law of first mention" as it pertains to salvation is first seen in Genesis 3:21: *"Unto Adam also and to his wife did the LORD God make coats of skins, and clothed them."* Here we learn three important requirements of salvation. First, salvation must be of the Lord. You can't create your own covering, atone for your sins, or get a new beginning without the Lord's provision. You cannot accomplish salvation through the works of your own hands or by good deeds. God is your only source.

Secondly, because the penalty for sin is death,

14

Life Is in the Blood

there must be the death of an innocent victim. The animal God killed in order to clothe Adam and Eve was innocent. It had not sinned, yet it was killed to atone for their sins.

Finally, salvation comes through the blood. The blood of the animal that was killed was shed in place of Adam's own blood. In other words, the animal became an innocent substitute for Adam and Eve. Later, God laid out the conditions for atonement by saying:

For the life of the flesh is in the blood: and I have given it to you upon the altar to make an atonement for your souls: for it is the blood that maketh an atonement for the soul (Leviticus 17:11).

Eventually these requirements led God to establish the Old Testament sacrifices and offerings that are recorded in Leviticus. These seven feasts and five offerings were the shadow of things to come in the New Testament (see Colossians 2:16,17).

The first four feasts—Passover, Unleavened Bread, Firstfruits, and Pentecost—foreshadow truths connected with the present gospel dispensation. (*Dake's Annotated Reference Bible* defines a *dispensation* as "a moral or probationary period in history in which God deals with men according to a particular test or responsibility, under which man is supposed to remain true to his trust of administering affairs for God under His direction.") The last three feasts—Trumpets, Atonement, and Tabernacles—foreshadow the blessings in store for God's chosen people, the Jews.

Before the law was given to Moses, people offered sacrifices to God but their effectiveness lay only in their faith. With the Mosaic Law came a pattern, order, and rules and regulations governing five different offerings—which, for the most part, were to be accomplished by priests appointed by God on behalf of the people:

- The *burnt offering* sacrificed the whole animal to God as a means of making personal consecration to the Lord (see Leviticus 6:22).
- The *peace offering* celebrated peace. It wasn't a plea for peace. It said, "Thank you, God, for the peace in my life." The meat from the offering was eaten by both the priest and the celebrants (Deuteronomy 12:18; 16:11).
- The *sin offering* was the only way to make restitution for offenses against God. It had to be done with a repentant heart or else forgiveness would not be given (see Numbers 15:30).
- Similar to the sin offering was the *trespass offering*. The trespass was committed out of ignorance. The difference between

Life Is in the Blood

trespass and sin offerings was that the trespass offering made restitution for an offense against both man and God (Leviticus 5:15).

- The *meal offering* (or the meat offering) was the only one that did not incorporate the sacrifice of an animal in and of itself, but it was always in conjunction with either a whole burnt offering or a peace offering. Presented as a meal to the Lord, it was symbolic of the best that humanity had to offer (see Leviticus 2). This was a consecration and praise for God's provisions.

The blood of all those sacrificial bulls and goats became a symbol of the ultimate sacrifice made by Jesus on the Cross: the animal's death in the place of the sinner symbolized the ultimate sacrifice by Jesus for man's sins. According to Hebrews 10:4, the blood or death of animals was not sufficient to take away sins. No matter how spotless or unblemished the animal was, its death was not an adequate propitiation or restitution for sin. That required the death of a spotless human life—the life of Jesus:

But Christ being come an high priest of good things to come, by a greater and more perfect tabernacle, not made with hands, that is to say, not of this building; Neither by the blood of goats and calves, but by his own blood he entered in once into the holy place, having obtained eternal redemption for us (Hebrews 9:11,12).

After the blood was shed, it was sprinkled on the priest's garments to sanctify his behavior in the Tabernacle and for the services (see Leviticus 8:10-12). Even the people to whom he ministered were sprinkled with the blood. The priest sprinkled blood outside the Tabernacle to protect the people who were entering it and applied blood to the horns of the golden altar before praying. Blood was sprinkled before the veil that separated the Holy of Holies from the rest of the Tabernacle before the priest entered on the day of atonement. (The Holy of Holies contained the Ark of the Covenant and the Mercy Seat.) The blood was the only thing that could protect the priest from God's judgment once inside. The blood applied to every area of his life.

As the priest progressed to the Mercy Seat, he sprinkled more blood in the holy place where the golden lampstand, table of shewbread, and golden altar of incense stood. Finally he applied blood to the Mercy Seat itself so that the judgment of God's law, which was placed underneath the Mercy Seat in the Ark of the Covenant, would not come upon the people who opened the Ark. When at last the Ark was opened, blood was sprinkled on the Book of the Covenant (which was as much of the Bible as was written at the time).

As Christians, we no longer have to go through all these rituals and ceremonies. Jesus is our Lamb. That means even the most lowly person in other men's eyes is worthy to enter into the presence of God without fear and trembling as long as he is covered by the blood of Jesus. When Jesus died, the veil was torn from top to bottom, allowing all Christians free access to the Father. Christ's blood covers your sins, protecting you from God's judgment.

In looking over the Scriptures, we see a progressive revelation of the blood. The first lamb was slain by Abel on behalf of himself (Genesis 4:4). The second lamb was slain by Noah for his family (Genesis 8:20). The third lamb was slain by many for a nation (Exodus 12:1-14). The last Lamb gave up His own life for the world (I Peter 1:18,19).

The Importance of the Blood Covenant

In Hebrew, the word for "covenant" is *berith*, which literally means "cut a compact (made by passing between pieces of flesh), confederacy, or league." In the Old Testament, the terms "cut" and "make" a covenant are used quite frequently. Both words come from the Hebrew word *karath*, which means "cut covenant, make a league," and "to be chewed."

Release the Power of the Blood Covenant

As we have already seen, God killed or "cut" an animal to clothe Adam and Eve, thereby cutting covenant with them. But, I must admit that when I first looked at these meanings, I was amazed at that last meaning, "to chew." I wondered, "How in the world can you 'chew' a covenant?" The Lord reminded me that many of the offerings or sacrifices made as part of covenants were often eaten by the participants. Even more importantly, the New Covenant of Jesus Christ is a "chewed" covenant! Jesus said:

*. . . Verily, verily, I say unto you, Except ye **eat** the flesh of the Son of man, and **drink** his blood, ye have no life in you. Whoso eateth my flesh, and drinketh my blood, hath eternal life; and I will raise him up at the last day. For my flesh is meat indeed, and my blood is drink indeed. He that eateth my flesh, and drinketh my blood, dwelleth in me, and I in him. As the living Father hath sent me, and I live by the Father: so he that eateth me, even he shall live by me. This is that bread which came down from heaven: not as your fathers did eat manna, and are dead: he that eateth of this bread shall live for ever* (John 6:53-58).

Tragically, after Jesus proclaimed this truth concerning the bread of life, many of his disciples left Him. It was just too hard a statement for them

Life Is in the Blood

to deal with. It wasn't that He asked them to actually become cannibals; the truth was that He asked them to join Him in a NEW covenant, one which would require them to leave behind the Temple and all the ritualistic offerings and sacrifices of the Old Covenant in exchange for new life in Him.

Jesus must have been greatly saddened because, after their departure, He turned to the 12 apostles and asked them if they were going to leave Him too. Peter responded:

. . . Lord, to whom shall we go? thou hast the words of eternal life. And we believe and are sure that thou art that Christ, the Son of the living God (John 6:68,69).

Hallelujah! Even before the New Covenant was "cut" by Jesus on the Cross, Peter grasped the core truths of the new birth: there is no one else to turn to for salvation, Christ is the only way to eternal life, Jesus is the Christ, and Jesus is the Son of the living God. These are the truths that every Christian acknowledges; these are the standards of the New Covenant.

The confession of these standards ratify our agreement to take part in the covenant. Yet few of us realize that it takes more than confessing belief in Jesus to establish this covenant. You see, Jesus tells us, *". . . in the mouth of two or three witnesses every word may be established"*

(Matthew 18:16).

Who, then, are the witnesses to this covenant? First of all, we see that the New Covenant is established by the Father, Son, and Holy Spirit. The Father is the maker, initiator, originator; the covenant maker and keeper. The Son, the second Person of the Trinity, sacrificed His body and blood to mediate the covenant. The Holy Spirit is the executor, appointed to carry out the will and the testament of the Father and Son. As the third Person of the Trinity, He is the completer and fulfiller of the covenant because He works in us to quicken and reveal the covenant to us. This means when we are in covenant relationship with the Lord, we don't just know Him; we know His Son Who shed His blood and the Holy Spirit Who reveals it to us.

Why did God initiate covenants with man in the first place? Some covenants are made for **security** purposes. This idea is especially easy to understand in a society where home security systems, security guards, and security monitors and alarms are a multi-million-dollar industry. A "covenant" for security purposes usually requires signing a contract which ensures that neither party will take advantage of the other. The company providing the security for your home has free access to the premises and can move about at will, while protecting those areas from unwelcome intruders. Security guards are bonded as an extra measure of security which says to you that they will not steal what they are protecting. Usually, your end of the agreement is as simple as signing a contract and handing over a check.

Love is another reason for cutting a covenant; this is especially true of the covenant of marriage. But a love covenant is not necessarily restricted to marriage. It can be made between friends. For example, David and Jonathan established a perfect example of a love covenant of friendship:

So Jonathan made a covenant with the house of David, . . . And Jonathan caused David to swear again, because he loved him: for he loved him as he loved his own soul (I Samuel 20:16,17).

A third reason is for **preservation**. Among tribal peoples, weaker tribes might covenant with a stronger tribe. This covenant would provide protection and enable the weaker tribe to preserve itself. Similarly, if Adam and Eve had not cut a covenant with God, they would not have survived. Their sin would have meant immediate death.

I once spoke to the wife of a Canadian missionary to Uganda. Several years ago, when Milton Obote (an ungodly dictator) came to power in Uganda, God told Gary and his wife that if they stayed there, He would protect them and their three children. And believe me, He protected

Release the Power of the Blood Covenant

them!

As Christians, they were in covenant relationship with God and claimed the power of the blood of Jesus to protect them. They told their children that God would take care of them; but they also prepared their children to meet Jesus. One night, 25 men tried to knock down their kitchen door while Gary's wife was alone with the three children. As the four of them huddled together under a bed, the 4-year-old was so scared she asked, "Mother, are we going to see Jesus tonight? Are we going to die?"

"How, did you answer that?" I asked.

"Well," she said, "God gives you the grace for the occasion. I couldn't answer her, so we just prayed."

And you know, 25 men couldn't knock down that door! God protected them. Why? Because of the blood.

But that's not all. She also told me about another time when some men broke in while they were eating dinner. One of the bandits put a gun to Gary's head and told him they wanted his money. Gary told them where the money was, but it wasn't enough to satisfy their greed. Gary insisted that was all the money they had, but the gunman didn't believe him and said he was going to kill him. He cocked the gun at Gary's head and pulled the trigger as his family looked on in horror.

Life Is in the Blood

God was faithful to His promise to them—the gun wouldn't go off. The gunman tried to shoot Gary again but nothing happened.

Finally, the gunman asked, "What are you, anyway?"

Gary said, "I'm a Christian."

"Oh," said the gunman, "that's the problem."

And they left! The blood makes a huge difference in the life of every believer who enters into covenant with God through the blood of Jesus Christ!

Christians have a covenant with God for all these reasons. However, covenant relationship with God gives them more than just divine protection, love, and security. It gives them redemption and eternal life. Yes, life is in the blood. And if you're a Christian, *your* life is in the blood—the blood of Jesus Christ.

Chapter Two
His Promises Are True

If you caught your child with his hand in the cookie jar, what would you do? Would you reprimand him and take the cookies away from him? Would you forbid him to ever do that again? Perhaps you would move the cookie jar to some place the child couldn't reach.

God saw His first children, Adam and Eve, when they blew it. Only instead of a cookie jar, they ate of the tree of knowledge of good and evil. It was no minor offense; what they did was a sin.

To understand the true seriousness of Adam and Eve's offense, we must first understand that God is a covenant-making and covenant-keeping God. With each covenant God initiated, He revealed a little bit more about Himself and what He had to offer man. Gradually we have come to know a righteous, loving God Who wants to bless us with all good things and takes delight in the happiness of His children.

Through studying God's nine covenants, we will learn God's will and purpose for man. We will see that each of the covenants initiated by God contains three main characteristics: (1) words or

Release the Power of the Blood Covenant

promises; (2) the shedding of blood to indicate that it was a life and death matter; and (3) a seal, sign, or token to remind them of the covenant.

The **words or promises** of the covenant were often recorded as blessings and curses and the conditions on which those blessings or curses would occur. These recorded words became the book of the covenant. When we look at the Bible we see that it is divided into two parts: the Old Testament and the New Testament. The Old Testament is the book of the Old Covenant; the New Testament is the book of the New Covenant.

We have already seen that the **shedding of blood** was an integral part of the covenant-making process. God said that life was in the blood so when a blood sacrifice was made, it represented the life commitment of those entering into the covenant.

The **seal** was a visible reminder to both parties of the words or promises of the covenant. Many times, children in this country are such good friends that they exchange prized possessions with one another so that whenever one child looks at the object that once belonged to his friend, he is reminded of the strength of that friendship pact they have made. That object then becomes a seal of their "covenant."

In many cases, the covenant was irrevocable. Once the people entered into the covenant, there

His Promises Are True

was nothing they could do to ever change it. The Constitution of the United States is the most enduring "covenant" of modern history. Yet legislators and government officials can make laws that "amend" the Constitution thus adding to the terms of the original agreement and changing its content. In the thousands of years man has been upon the earth, though, there has never been a covenant with God that has been changed or altered in any way.

God initiates a covenant by calling individuals to come to Him. When they respond and enter into the covenant, they agree to the terms and conditions of the covenant. However, the hardest part for mankind has always been the keeping of the covenant. Yet, despite the fact that God is a covenant-enabling God, man has broken covenant after covenant.

When man broke the terms of a covenant, God would initiate another one. Each covenant God made with man was foreordained. God knew before man was ever created that he would sin. So He devised a series of covenants to insure man's redemption from sin and restore communion with Him. Through these covenants we can truly come to know and understand Him. So let's look at each of the Old Testament covenants and see how they were fulfilled in the New Testament.

The Edenic Covenant

The Edenic Covenant was made before the entrance of sin. It revealed God's original purpose for man and for Creation. After the heavens and the earth were formed, He filled them with beauty. He prepared everything that man would need to sustain life **before** He created man. Then God made man in His own image:

And God said, Let us make man in our image, after our likeness: .... So God created man in his own image, in the image of God created he him; ... (Genesis 1:26,27).

Revelation 4:11 says God created us for His pleasure. Then He set Adam into the Garden of Eden so that Adam could get to know Him intimately. From the beginning, God wanted a close, intimate relationship with us. He had, and will always have, a hunger to know us in the way we relate to Him.

God's purposes in creating man formed the words or promises of the Edenic Covenant. The blessings that accompanied these promises were dependant on Adam carrying out these responsibilities:

And God blessed them, and God said unto them, Be fruitful, and multiply, and replenish the earth, and subdue it: and have dominion over the fish of the sea, and over the fowl of the air, and over every living thing that moveth upon the earth (Genesis 1:28).

Notice that God told Adam to "subdue" the earth. According to *Strong's Exhaustive Concordance*, "subdue" means "to conquer." Since this instruction was given before sin entered the world (and the curse that followed it), the Lord must have been telling Adam and Eve to conquer Satan—the only thing that needed to be conquered.

If Adam was to obey God's command to replenish the earth, he would need a wife. God put Adam into the sleep of death and took out one of his ribs to form Eve. Genesis 2:21 says God, "*. . . closed up the flesh instead thereof.*" It took the cutting of flesh and the shedding of blood to produce Adam's bride. Likewise, Jesus' side was pierced while He was on the Cross. His death and resurrection produced the Church—His bride!

Adam and Eve were told to reproduce after their own kind. I believe God wanted them to produce a race of godly people who would know, love, and serve God. As Christians, we have the same responsibility to our children. We need to do more than just raise our children; we need to train them in the things of the Lord.

God gave Adam and Eve only one command to obey: they were not to eat the fruit of the tree of knowledge of good and evil:

And the LORD God commanded the man,

saying, Of every tree of the garden thou mayest freely eat: But of the tree of the knowledge of good and evil, thou shalt not eat of it: for in the day that thou eatest thereof thou shalt surely die (Genesis 2:16,17).

Both the tree of life and the tree of knowledge of good and evil were in the middle of the garden. The tree of life was the seal of the Edenic Covenant; it was a sign of Adam and Eve's never-ending life with God. The tree of knowledge of good and evil symbolized the curse; if they ate of it, Adam and Eve would not live forever but die.

Satan came to this same spot in the garden to tempt Eve. First he approached her with a question that led Eve to doubt what God had said. Look at how Eve answered when Satan asked her if God allowed them to eat of all the trees:

*And the woman said unto the serpent, We may eat of the fruit of the trees of the garden: But of the fruit of the tree which is in the midst of the garden, God hath said, Ye shall not eat of it, **neither shall ye touch it**, lest ye die* (Genesis 3:2,3).

God never said Adam and Eve weren't supposed to *touch* the tree. Satan tempted Eve to become like God when she was already made in His image and likeness. Had she responded to Satan with the Word the way Jesus did when he tempted Him, she could have overcome temptation; but she

His Promises Are True

didn't. She ate the fruit and passed it on to Adam to eat.

Adam and Eve knew immediately the effects of their sin. Before the fall, their world revolved around God; now they had entered a world apart from God. He created them to be dependent on Him; now their fellowship with God was severed.

When they chose to eat the fruit of the forbidden tree, they turned their backs on God. Sin not only brought on the curse of death, but they lost their authority over Satan. That necessitated a new covenant of redemption which would ultimately restore to mankind what was lost in the fall.

Chapter Three
Old Testament Covenants

Adam and Eve were in a horrible position! Imagine their feelings of hopelessness after they sinned! They must have been horrified at the realization of what they had done, but God was not taken by surprise. Even though disobedience to God is the basic sin of man, God is merciful.

The redemptive covenants that followed the Edenic Covenant highlight specific areas of blessings that our heavenly Father wanted to give men if they chose and obeyed Him.

The Adamic Covenant

The first of these redemptive covenants is the Adamic Covenant, which reveals God's plan of redemption and the judgment of sin. It also reveals the curses that would come upon man, woman, Satan, and the snake. The snake, used by Satan as part of his plan to destroy God's creation, was cursed to eat dust and crawl on its belly forever. The curse upon Satan was everlasting: he would eventually be totally and utterly destroyed by the seed of the woman. God told Eve that women would experience pain and sorrow in carrying out

Release the Power of the Blood Covenant

God's original commandment to be fruitful and replenish the earth and man would rule over her. Adam reaped a curse upon himself of toil, pain, sweat, and death. God cursed the earth to make it difficult to till. Both spiritual death (separation from God) and physical death would result.

At the same time, and even more importantly, God gave Adam and Eve the hope and promise of a coming Messiah:

And I will put enmity between thee [Satan] *and the woman, and between thy seed and her seed; it shall bruise thy head, and thou shalt bruise his heel* (Genesis 3:15).

Women do not carry seed. Yet this scripture refers to the seed of the woman which would crush Satan's head. That seed is Jesus, our virgin-born Savior Who spoiled Satan by conquering principalities, powers, and rulers of darkness. Satan bruised His heel because he saw to it that Jesus was crucified. So we see that God's commitment to mankind was a commitment unto death—the death of His only Son. When Jesus died on the Cross, believers also benefited from that promise—Satan is under our feet as well.

God confirmed this covenant with Adam and Eve through the shedding of blood and sealed it with the skins of animals. He killed an animal to clothe Adam and Eve: *"Unto Adam also and to his wife did the LORD God make coats of skins, and clothed them*" (Genesis 3:21). Until this point, Adam and Eve had never even seen death. For the first time they felt the sting of death and, perhaps, the grief over the loss of an animal who had been their friend. The institution of animal sacrifices came to be a reminder to people of their coming Redeemer Who would shed His own blood as a sacrifice for the redemption of mankind.

When God took the skin to clothe Adam and Eve, the skin became a covering—a sign of the promised covering for sin. There was no way to get back into fellowship with God and make an atonement for sin except through the shedding of blood. There had to be another Adam, perfect in every way and totally sinless before a perfect sacrifice could be made for the redemption of sins.

God had to expel Adam and Eve from the Garden of Eden. If He hadn't, they would have had access to the tree of life, eaten of its fruit, and lived forever in their sins. The righteousness of God could not tolerate that, so He placed angels to guard the entrance to Eden. No more could man enter there and commune intimately with God.

The Noahic Covenant

I'm sure Adam and Eve probably worked from sunup to sundown tilling the hard earth. Coming home tired and exhausted, they labored to make a nice home for their two sons, Cain and Abel.

They no doubt raised their boys in the nurture and admonition of the Lord, teaching them that atonement for their sins came only through blood sacrifices. Despite their efforts, sin reared its ugly head and Cain killed his brother.

From that point on sin gained momentum. People had no regard for life or God. They were divided into believers and unbelievers, the godly and the ungodly. The law of sin took total control and drove man further from God. It got so bad, God decided to destroy His creation.

Despite the ungodly ways of mankind, there was still one man left who followed after God: *"But Noah found grace in the eyes of the Lord"* (Genesis 6:8). So God revealed His plans for the coming flood to Noah and revealed to him a way of escape for himself, his family, and pairs of every living creature. God also established a covenant with him:

But with thee will I establish my covenant; and thou shalt come into the ark, thou, and thy sons, and thy wife, and thy sons' wives with thee (Genesis 6:18).

It took Noah 100 years to build the ark following God's very specific instructions. During that time, Noah preached to the people, calling them to repentance, but they only scorned and mocked him.

Noah *never* saw any fruit even after 100 years

Old Testament Covenants

of preaching, witnessing, and praying for them. So when the ark was finished, God brought all the animals into it, secured Noah and his family inside, and closed the door. For the next 40 days and nights it rained so much that the only living things left upon the earth were those who were in the ark.

God brought Noah and his family safely through the flood. Noah must have heard the cries of people screaming for rescue, though it was too late. For them, there was only judgment; but for Noah there was a covenant of protection and of the future promised Deliverer. God has established a covenant of protection with us, too.

When Noah and his family finally emerged from the ark, Noah built an altar and offered a sacrifice to God which became the blood of the Noahic Covenant. When God smelled the sweet savor, He set forth the promise of the Noahic Covenant: He would never destroy the earth again with a flood, the seasons were established, and day and night would not cease. God had instructed them not to eat blood but now they could eat meat; and He instituted capital punishment for murderers (see Genesis 8:21-9:11).

God then proceeded to bless Noah and his family and gave them the same commandment He had originally given to Adam and Eve: *"And God blessed Noah and his sons, and said unto them,*

Be fruitful, and multiply, and replenish the earth" (Genesis 9:1). Unfortunately, later a curse came upon the descendants of Ham, who had discovered that his son, Canaan, had committed a sexual act with Noah when he was drunk. Ham dishonored his father by exposing the sin (Genesis 9:20-27), and Noah cursed Canaan. On the other hand, Noah's son, Shem, was blessed because he covered his father's sin—the promised Messiah would come through Shem.

God also gave mankind the rainbow as an everlasting sign of the Noahic covenant. A study of the rainbow proves very interesting. There is a rainbow around the throne of God (Revelation 4:3) and another around the head of Jesus (Revelation 10:1). Whenever God looks upon a rainbow, He is reminded of His promise in the Noahic Covenant and we can be confident that God will not judge the earth again by a flood.

The Abrahamic Covenant

Noah lived long enough to see the rebirth of nations upon the earth. Unfortunately, he also saw the rebirth of sin in the hearts of men beginning with his own family. Though Noah remained faithful to the covenant, his sons did not. As Noah's descendants reproduced, mankind returned to its old sinful ways. Following man's failure at the tower of Babel (see Genesis 11:1-9),

Old Testament Covenants

God confounded man's language and scattered them around the earth. This could have been a fatal blow to mankind but God specializes in restoration, and His covenants always included provision for man's inability to keep his end of the agreement.

When the Noahic Covenant was broken, God established a new covenant with Abram, a descendant of Shem. Abram had no inherent goodness—he worshiped idols—yet something caused God to seek him out to be the father of a new nation. That something was grace. This is true for us today. Jesus told us that He was the Good Shepherd and that He would go after His sheep *". . . according to the election of grace"* (Romans 11:5).

Because of the idolatry that surrounded Abram, Abram needed to separate himself from all the ungodly influences. Abram left his home in Ur and walked in faith and obedience all the way to Canaan—about a 1,000-mile journey. God didn't tell him where he was going; all He said was that He would show him a land. When Abram obeyed, God counted his faith as righteousness and later sealed the covenant through the rite of circumcision. Every male would have his foreskin removed as a physical sign of his covenant relationship with God. While the New Covenant circumcision is not external, it is one of the heart—at the new birth we cut off the fleshly life, and walk in the nature of Jesus Christ. And like Abraham, we get new names too; we're called *Christians,* followers of Christ.

The promises of the Abrahamic Covenant unfolded over a span of time. Genesis 12:2,3 tells us the first part: God would make Abram a great nation and bless all the families of the earth through him and his seed (the Messiah came from Abram's seed). The second part of the covenant was confirmed after Abram returned from Egypt following a famine. God spoke to Abram and told him that all the land that he could see would be his and his seed's forever and that his seed would be innumerable. God told Abram to walk through the land that would be his. This then became the land grant for his natural seed.

Not only did Abram's faith count for righteousness, it also identified him as the friend of God. His friendship gave him the courage to boldly remind God of His promise of innumerable seed. Abram was an old man at this point. God must have sympathized with him because He told him that his seed would be as innumerable as the stars. Later, when Abram was 99 years old, God appeared to him, calling Himself by a new name, "God Almighty"—and Abram's covenant name became "Abraham." Then God named their yet-to-be-born son, Isaac. The following year,

Abraham and his wife, Sarah, were the proud parents of a healthy baby boy, the seed of promise.

Abraham was faithful so God gave him a multitude of blessings! Even the curse of the Abrahamic Covenant is actually a blessing—anyone who curses Abraham or his seed will be cursed by God (see Genesis 12:3).

When God gives great blessing, there will be testing. So God tested Abraham. He told Abraham to offer Isaac to Him as a sacrifice. Setting out to obey God, Abraham prepared to offer Isaac, never doubting that even if he killed Isaac, God would raise him up again. God was so impressed with Abraham's faith that He enlarged the Abrahamic Covenant:

That in blessing I will I will bless thee, and in multiplying I will multiply thy seed as the stars of the heaven and as the sand which is upon the sea shore; and thy seed shall possess the gate of the enemies; And in thy seed shall all the nations of the earth be blessed; because thou hast obeyed my voice (Genesis 22:17,18).

The Mosaic Covenant

The promises of the Abrahamic Covenant were passed down to Abraham's seed through Isaac and Jacob. Abraham's seed increased greatly after Jacob followed Joseph to Egypt. During the 400 years the Hebrews spent in Egypt, their number

Release the Power of the Blood Covenant

increased to about 2 million and, again, the God of their fathers was forgotten—they turned to the idols of Egypt. They were no longer in covenant relationship with God and so the fierceness of the wrath of the Egyptians was poured out on them. Finally, they began to cry unto God for a redeemer.

God chose Moses as Israel's deliverer. God performed all kinds of miracles to deliver the Hebrews from Egypt, and He did miracles for them while they were in the wilderness. He prepared them to take the land He had promised them in the Abrahamic Covenant, but they repeatedly failed their test of faith and provoked God.

God put the nation of Israel on "probation." It was during the 40 years in the wilderness that God initiated the Mosaic Covenant. Unlike the other covenants which were made with individuals, God initiated the Mosaic Covenant with His chosen people—the nation of Israel. He gave them a covenant of law and works to reveal to them their inability to obey Him apart from His grace.

The words of the Mosaic Covenant became the law which was divided into three parts: the moral law (the Ten Commandments), the civil law (which governed daily living and social situations), and ceremonial law (which had to do with their relationship with God and with others). In keeping the law through faith and obedience, the Hebrews were blessed with personal, national, geographic,

Old Testament Covenants

and spiritual blessings. These blessings were actually affirmations of the promises God made in the Abrahamic Covenant. (See Exodus 23:25-33 and Leviticus 25 and 26 for a complete breakdown of all these blessings.)

All the blessings were conditional; most started with *"if."* "If" they didn't adhere to the conditions of that blessing, a curse would come. For example, Exodus 23:33 says, *". . . if thou serve their gods, it will surely be a snare unto thee."* All of the conditions, blessings, and curses are recorded in the book of the covenant, which is actually the entire Pentateuch. This covenant incorporated all the previous covenant's blessings with all the laws, rules, and regulations God gave them to govern every area of Israel's life.

It is extremely important to understand that this covenant is directed specifically to the nation of Israel in order to give the people a divine standard of righteousness. God wanted them to have a clear definition of sin because they had no sin consciousness.

When the Israelites "cut" the covenant, the book of the covenant was read to the congregation of Israel and they all agreed to its terms. Then the blood of this covenant was shed through an elaborate sacrificial system illustrating that no amount of animal sacrifices could effectively take away man's sinfulness. Also, it pointed to Christ's once-and-for-all sacrifice that would take away the sin of the world (Hebrews 9,10). It was the multiple sacrifices that caused the Mosaic Covenant to become known as the "blood covenant" (see Exodus 24:6-8).

The seal of the Mosaic Covenant was the Sabbath. This seal was fulfilled in the New Covenant. The word *Sabbath* means "rest," and believers find eternal rest in Christ Jesus. Instead of writing the laws and rules that we are to live by on tablets of stone, Jesus writes the new law on our heart. And what is that law? To simply love God and your neighbor as yourself.

The Palestinian Covenant

The Palestinian Covenant was a land grant covenant. Its focus was the Promised Land; it governed the Israelites' entrance into the land God was going to give them and set up conditions for living in the land once they took it. This land grant was specifically to Abraham's descendants and does not apply to Abraham's spiritual seed.

Because of the failure of the "wilderness generation" to keep covenant—and especially because of their unbelief regarding Joshua and Caleb's statement that they could take the land—God established the Palestinian Covenant with the second-generation Israelites on the plains of Moab. Although Moses couldn't accompany them into

Old Testament Covenants

the Promised Land, he did give them the words of the covenant which is the book of Deuteronomy. It took nearly a month to read the terms and conditions, the blessings and curses of this covenant.

Deuteronomy 8,11,26,28 and Leviticus 25 and 26 record the promises, blessings, and curses of the Palestinian Covenant. Its promises relate to the beauty, geography, and fruitfulness of the Promised Land. God told them that they would inherit all that belonged to the idolatrous people who inhabited the land and that they'd eat what they didn't plant. They would be blessed in the city and the field; their daily provisions would be taken care of; everything they put their hand to would prosper, and they wouldn't lack for anything.

God imposed certain conditions on the Israelites; not only did they have to keep the terms of the Mosaic Covenant, they would also have to respect the land in order for the blessings to overtake them. Every seventh year the land was to have a rest. Then every 50 years was a year of jubilee where both the people and the land could rest.

These Sabbaths became the seal of the Palestinian Covenant. God promised tremendous prosperity in the years prior to jubilee so the peoples' needs would be met during the jubilee year. He promised to send the early and latter rains as His seal upon the land. If they failed to honor the land's Sabbath, He would not send the rains, and curses would overtake them.

When the Israelites crossed the Jordan into the Promised Land, they built an altar and sacrificed burnt offerings and peace offerings to God. The blood that was shed on that altar became the blood of the Palestinian Covenant, and I believe, formed its eastern border.

The Davidic Covenant

The Israelites had been in the Promised Land for approximately 400 years by the time David ascended to the throne. God had told them He would be their King and the Israelites would be His kingdom of priests. Yet, Israel wasn't satisfied with what God was offering them. They wanted to be ruled over by kings like the other nations. God didn't want them to be like everyone else. He wanted them to show the rest of the world what it was like to be in covenant with God almighty so the world would turn to Him.

Even though they rejected God by wanting a king, He permitted Saul to reign over them. Saul had everything going for him. He was tall and good looking; and God had given him a new heart and the presence of the Holy Spirit. He even had an anointed prophet to minister to him. At first Saul was quite humble; but as time went by, Saul began to exalt himself. So God chose a man after His own heart to succeed Saul. That "man" was David, a simple shepherd boy.

David was far from perfect. Though he sinned, he knew that God didn't just want sacrifices to relieve the burden of his sins. He knew that God wanted a broken and contrite heart (see Psalms 51:16,17). Above all else, David desired fellowship with God.

David's undying devotion led God to establish a covenant with him. Much like the Abrahamic Covenant, the Davidic Covenant was revealed in stages. The first stage concerned David's kingship—foreshadowing of the coming King of kings. Years before Saul's death, God told Samuel to anoint David king and to offer a sacrifice, thereby shedding the blood of this covenant (see I Samuel 16:2-13).

The second stage came following David's unification of the country of Israel. David knew the promises of the land grant given to Israel through preceding covenants, and he became consumed with doing what God had told the Hebrews to do when they entered the Promised Land—he drove out those who were not in covenant relationship with his God.

When David succeeded and brought peace to the country, his all-consuming love for God prompted him to bring the Ark of the Covenant to Jerusalem at which time he also offered burnt offerings and peace offerings before the Lord (see II Samuel 6:17,18). David's ultimate desire in bringing the Ark to Jerusalem was to build a house for God; but in the end, God told David that his son, Solomon, would build the Temple and God would build a house for David. In II Samuel 7:11-16 we see the full extent of the promise of the Davidic Covenant:

. . . the LORD telleth thee that he will make thee an house. And when thy days be fulfilled, and thou shalt sleep with thy fathers, I will set up thy seed after thee, which shall proceed out of thy bowels, and I will establish his kingdom. He shall build an house for my name, and I will stablish the throne of his kingdom for ever. I will be his father, and he shall be my son. If he commit iniquity, I will chasten him with the rod of men, and with the stripes of the children of men: But my mercy shall not depart away from him, as I took it from Saul, whom I put away before thee. And thine house and thy kingdom shall be established for ever before thee: thy house shall be established for ever before thee: thy throne shall be established for ever.

Even though the word "covenant" was not mentioned, both David and God knew it was a covenant. David's last words referred to his covenant with God: *"'Truly is not my house so with God? For He has made an everlasting covenant with me, Ordered in all things, and secured; ... '"* (II Samuel 23:5, NAS). In this aspect of the covenant lies the most important promise; the Messiah would come through the lineage of David. David's kingdom was maintained until Jesus came through David's seed. Because Jesus is the permanent King, the scepter never departed from the household of David.

Though this covenant has no specific curse attached to it, God commanded David and his seed to walk in faith and obedience. When a Davidic king disobeyed God's Word, rather than break His oath concerning the eternal reign of David's seed, God simply transferred the throne to another descendant who would be obedient.

The best summary of the Davidic Covenant is found in Psalms 89. David reviews the terms of this covenant in verses 19-37. These verses also contain the seal of the Davidic Covenant:

*My covenant will I not break, nor alter the thing that is gone out of my lips. Once have I sworn by my holiness that I will not lie unto David. His seed shall endure for ever, and his throne as the **sun** before me. It shall be established for ever as the **moon**, and as a faithful witness in heaven....* (Psalms 89:34-37).

Release the Power of the Blood Covenant

Do you see it? The sun and moon seal the Davidic Covenant! As long as these reflectors of light continue to function—until eternity comes and the light from the glory of God and Jesus lights our way in the New Jerusalem—the throne of David will continue through the Kingship of Jesus. Every time we gaze at the heavens, we should be reminded that Jesus is the light of the world!

Chapter Four
Forever and Ever

Silence prevailed. Not a word, not a prophecy, nothing. God wasn't speaking. The 400 years between the time of the Old Testament and the time of the New Testament must have seemed inordinately long to the Jewish nation because they hadn't heard even a peep from God since their return from Babylon.

After the death of David, a series of mostly ungodly kings ruled over Israel's divided kingdom. For 490 years, the Israelites had not followed the terms of their covenants; the Sabbaths hadn't been observed, and the people had fallen into idolatry. Because they failed to keep the covenant, they were taken into exile by the Babylonians for 70 years—one year of exile for every land Sabbath they had not kept. There they learned their lesson. Upon their return to Israel, the Israelites committed themselves to keeping the covenant. Unfortunately, the letter of the law became the established norm and instead of becoming a godly nation, they were becoming a "Jewish" nation.

The New Covenant

It was at this point in history that Jesus came to establish a New Covenant. The Jews had managed to stick to the terms of the Old Covenant religiously for hundreds of years and had not fallen back into idol worship. They kept waiting for their long-promised Messiah, but when He came, they resisted Him and His New Covenant.

Jesus' New Covenant was written in His blood, and the Jews could not understand this. He talked to them of eating His flesh and drinking His blood—a concept completely forbidden by the Old Covenant. They could not understand that the Old Covenant was supposed to prepare them for the New—which was the promised Redeemer—and so they rejected Him.

Fulfilling the Old Covenant, Jesus bought us a covenant of love: *"Greater love hath no man than this, that a man lay down his life for his friends"* (John 15:13). God knew that only Jesus could fulfill all the terms of the Old Covenant, and so He sent His only Son to die for us, the last Lamb slain upon an altar for the sins of man. Jesus' sacrifice was the ultimate sacrifice; further sacrifices are no longer required by God.

The promises of blessings and curses, the conditions and terms, and the seal of the New Covenant are all recorded in the New Testament. The promises are much better than those in the previous covenants, and through faith in Jesus Christ, believers can receive all the wonderful New Covenant blessings. We'll study more about these blessings in subsequent chapters, but for now let me just name some of them: forgiveness, justification, adoption, sanctification, assurance, healing, glorification, and the outpouring of the Holy Spirit.

In contrast to the wonderful blessings, the curses of this covenant are often enough to make believers out of men! As we've already seen, the majority of the Jewish people rejected their Messiah. Their rejection resulted in a terrible curse which was pictured in Jesus' cursing of the fig tree: cursed to its roots, the fig would never again bear fruit. So it is that Israel was cursed as a nation. This curse, however, is not just limited to Israel. Any nation that rejects Jesus is cursed and anyone whose name is not listed in the Lamb's book of life will experience eternal judgment.

The blood that Jesus shed on the Cross is the most precious, holy thing to have ever been spilled on the earth. It alone can reconcile man to the Father. It alone can give eternal life and eternal redemption for believers. Only the blood of Christ can turn man's heart to the heart of God because it resides in heaven forever crying, "Mercy, mercy," for the sins of man.

The Holy Spirit testifies that Jesus' one sacrifice,

one covenant, was and always will be sufficient to sanctify men to God; and in so doing, the Holy Spirit becomes the seal of the New Covenant:

Whereof the Holy Ghost also is a witness to us: for after that he had said before, This is the covenant that I will make with them after those days, saith the Lord, I will put my laws into their hearts, and in their minds will I write them; And their sins and iniquities will I remember no more. Now where remission of these is, there is no more offering for sin (Hebrews 10:15-18).

The outpouring of the blood was followed by the outpouring of the Spirit. Because of the Holy Spirit, every believer is sealed into this covenant. We are born again by the Holy Spirit, and then He comes to dwell in the hearts of men. We are now enabled to pray more effectively; witness more boldly; and can rest assured that we have an everlasting, irrevocable, life-giving Covenant. The blood covenant of Jesus Christ makes us priests and kings. And even if we blow it, Jesus is our Advocate, ever-living to make intercession for us to the Father.

The Everlasting Covenant

Even though the Everlasting Covenant is the last one we will study, it was actually the first one to be initiated! This covenant was not made **with** man but **for** man before time ever began. It was established among all three parties of the Godhead and encompasses all the covenants we have already looked at. It was designed to ensure that God's eternal purpose for mankind (Genesis 1:26-28) will be accomplished. Through the Everlasting Covenant, we are perfected in God's image; and we will subdue and have dominion over the earth and all its inhabitants.

The words of this covenant are the words of the entire Bible. All the "everlastings" are the promises and curses of this covenant. The promises and curses of all the other covenants are merely shadows of the eternal words in the Everlasting Covenant. The major promise, however, is eternal life (Titus 1:2); but there are also promises of eternal love, kindness, mercy, joy, strength, and victory to overcomers.

The Everlasting Covenant certainly contains the greatest curse of all. The "mother of all curses" will be executed at the Great White Throne judgment where eternal damnation will await unbelievers—those who reject God's redemptive covenant through Christ will be condemned at the Great White Throne Judgment (Revelation 20:11) and cast into hell where there is everlasting punishment, destruction, shame, contempt, and a lake of fire and brimstone.

The blood for this timeless covenant was shed

by the Lamb of God Who was slain before the foundation of the world (I Peter 1:19,20; Revelation 13:8). Christ's pure and sinless blood was poured out as the cleansing agent for sin; and right now, it is in heaven for us as the blood of the Everlasting Covenant (Hebrews 9:11-28; 10:19; 13:20).

The terms of the covenant are faith (John 3:16), love (John 14:15), and obedience (Hebrews 5:8). In addition, God made an oath that said after Christ's death, the Father would resurrect Him and give Him eternal priesthood after the order of Melchizedek (Hebrews 7:20-25). The book of this covenant is the "Lamb's Book of Life," which contains the names of all those who have been redeemed by the blood of Jesus (Revelation 3:5; 13:8; 22:19).

Just as in the New Covenant, the seal of the Everlasting Covenant is the Holy Spirit (Ephesians 1:13,14; 4:30). Christians are sealed, and our bodies will be glorified and made immortal when Jesus returns and the Church is raptured. We will be ushered into everlasting life, shining more brightly than the sun, moon, and stars; and we will rule and reign with Jesus forever.

Chapter Five
Your Spiritual Blood Line

We are beautifully and wonderfully made! Every cell serves a purpose. Bones, muscles, tendons, and joints work together to give us unique physical abilities. All the systems and organs in our bodies, though basically independent of each other, are interconnected through the brain—the body's control center. Yet, if it weren't for the blood, none of these actions and reactions, functions, and organs could do the job they were designed to do and we would die.

When God created Adam and Eve, their bodies were perfect in every way. Since they were made in the image and likeness of God, I believe their blood was pure and holy, just like God's. It carried no sickness or disease because sin hadn't entered the world yet.

All that changed when they sinned. Sin introduced "blood poisoning" into their systems! If it wasn't for blood poisoning, man could have lived forever. That same poisoning became an inheritance to all mankind because we are all related by the blood. No matter your nationality or ethnic background, there's sin in your blood.

Release the Power of the Blood Covenant

Acts 17:26 tells us God:
> *. . . hath made of one blood all nations of men for to dwell on all the face of the earth, . . .*

God had to do something about this blood poisoning in order to carry out His redemptive covenants with man. We've already seen that, even before Creation, the Trinity established the Everlasting Covenant which in turn led to the redemptive covenants. God knew His Son Jesus was going to be sent to earth to be born, live, and die as a man. But how was He going to overcome the problem with sin in the blood of man? If Jesus was going to be born human, His blood would be poisoned, too. And the only way for redemption to occur was to sacrifice the sinless blood of an innocent victim. God's solution was for Jesus to be virgin born:

> *And I will put enmity between thee and the woman, and between thy seed and her seed; it shall bruise thy head, and thou shalt bruise his heel* (Genesis 3:15).

The seed comes from a man; for a child to be the "seed" of a woman, the conception could not include a human male. You see, the baby's blood is inherited from its father. Once the egg is fertilized, the "blood gene" from the father's seed begins to manufacture and establish the baby's blood system. According to the *Nurses Handbook* of *Obstetrics*, at no point in any stage of fetal development does the mother's blood come into contact with the baby's blood system.

If Jesus were conceived through a man's seed, His blood would have been contaminated. But we know that it was God's blood that pumped through Jesus' heart and veins because the Holy Spirit came upon Mary, the power of the Highest overshadowed her, and she conceived the Son of God (see Luke 1:35). Jesus' blood doesn't contain the sin principle; it is incorruptible—it will never die or decay and nothing can ever cause it to stop giving life:

Forasmuch as ye know that ye were not redeemed with corruptible things, as silver and gold, . . . But with the precious blood of Christ, as of a lamb without blemish and without spot: Being born again, not of corruptible seed, but of incorruptible, by the word of God, which liveth and abideth for ever (I Peter 1:18,19,23).

A Supernatural Blood Transfusion

It takes life to stop death. Because death is a result of sin, only God's provision can restore life to mankind. That provision is Jesus. When you enter into covenant relationship with Him by symbolically partaking of His flesh and drinking His blood, you are given a new life, a new beginning. You are born again.

The blood of Jesus is important to all Christians. Though containing the same properties as the blood which flows through our veins, Jesus' shed blood carries with it new life. When we accept Jesus as our Lord and Savior, we accept His blood and all that it does for us. I call that a "spiritual blood transfusion," and without it we would die in our trespasses and sins.

Blood transfusions have tremendous power. A medical missionary to India once wrote of the transformation that occurred in his life when he saw what a blood transfusion could do. His father had been a missionary and was required to take some medical courses to better minister to the people. His son hated helping his father because he often had to help lance a boil or deliver a baby; and seeing all that blood made him sick. After cleaning up after a particularly gory incident, this young man made a decision that he would never become a doctor. A missionary, yes. A doctor, no. He associated blood with death and wanted no part in it.

While he was away at school in England, his father died, and his mother came to visit. She told him that his father always hoped he would become a medical missionary, and his uncle had agreed to pay his way. But he refused. He would go as a missionary but not as a *medical* missionary.

In order to go to India, he had to take the same

basic medical courses his father had taken. One night during his training, a dying woman was brought into the emergency room. Her skin was translucent; there was no color in her face; she couldn't move, hear, or open her eyes. The doctor on duty decided to give her a transfusion. As the transfusion started, this young man watched an immediate change come over this woman. Color returned to her face within seconds. She began to move. And then she opened her eyes and spoke.

He had seen the power of blood make a difference between life and death for that woman. At that point, God spoke to him and told him He wanted him to be a medical missionary. He obeyed God, because he saw that the blood brought life, and countless others' lives were saved as a result.

Your Paternal Inheritance

Because Jesus' blood was "inherited" from His Father, His blood brings life to us in more ways than one. To grasp the power that is available to us through the blood of Jesus, I want to compare the physical facts about human blood (the maternal side of the "family" so-to-speak) to the supernatural facts about Jesus' blood (the Paternal side). I think it helps us to understand the invisible by looking at the visible; and the physical qualities of blood provide a stunning picture of all the spiritual realities we can enjoy because of the shed blood of Jesus, our "Great Physician."

First of all, blood cleanses. Blood contains hemoglobin, which removes waste from every cell in the body. If there is not enough hemoglobin in the blood, toxins stay in the blood and cause sickness. Likewise, Jesus' blood carries away the waste of sin in your life. Through the blood of Jesus, God can bring about a real and living cleansing. The cleansing power of the Lord's blood purifies your heart from the inside out, and you can become spiritually sick if you do not stay washed in the blood of Jesus:

But if we walk in the light, as he is in the light, we have fellowship one with another, and **the blood of Jesus Christ his Son cleanseth us from all sin.** *If we confess our sins, he is faithful and just to forgive us our sins,* **and to cleanse us from all unrighteousness** (I John 1:7,9).

As the blood moves through your body, it carries nutrients and oxygen to the body's cells. There are millions of cells in your body, yet each cell receives new life through the blood more than once a minute. Through the blood of Jesus, you have a full supply of abundant life. From the moment you became born again, the life of God became your life:

Whoso eateth my flesh, and drinketh my blood, hath eternal life; and I will raise him up at the last day. He that eateth my flesh, and drinketh my blood, dwelleth in me, and I in him . . . . he that eateth of this bread shall live for ever (John 6:54,56,57).

Just as human blood controls your body temperature, Jesus' blood prevents your spiritual temperature from growing cold: *"And because iniquity shall abound, the love of many shall wax cold"* (Matthew 24:12). The passage of the blood through your body controls and maintains your temperature at a constant 98.6 degrees; your temperature doesn't depend on the body's external environment, but on the blood inside.

Because of the blood covenant, your Christian life doesn't depend on how others treat you. Rather, your Christian life is regulated and controlled by the blood of Christ working in you. Recognizing what the blood has done will raise your spiritual temperature.

When the blood is healthy, it provides energy to the body. Anemics know what it's like not to have any energy. They must stick to certain iron-rich diets and take vitamins and mineral supplements to give them energy. You need Christ's blood for energy too. It motivates you and provokes you to good works:

Having therefore, brethren, boldness to enter into the holiest by the blood of Jesus, By a new and living way, which he hath consecrated for us, . . . And let us consider one another to provoke unto love and to good works (Hebrews 10:19,20,24).

Natural blood carries adrenaline and other hormones to critical parts of the body to help you respond quickly and effectively in emergencies. Adrenaline is distributed throughout the blood stream and turns ordinary people into "superhumans"; a classic example is a 100-pound mother lifting a car off her child.

Jesus' blood is your 9-1-1 connection to God. When you have an emergency or hit a spiritual crisis, the blood of Jesus can rescue you. His blood can provide you with supernatural power to help you overcome any obstacle: *"And they overcame him by the blood of the Lamb, and by the word of their testimony; . . . "* (Revelation 12:11).

Your blood contains millions of white blood cells (leucocytes) which are the body's front-line troops in fighting infection. The white cells look like fried eggs sprinkled with pepper. Those little "pepper spots" are actually weapons that fight disease. When a disease or sickness attacks your body, about 24 million white cells are sent to the site to battle it. Another 24 million or so cling to the sides of capillaries, veins, and arteries protecting them from the infestation.

As a Christian, you can claim the blood of Jesus as your first line of defense in spiritual attacks. When the death angel passed over Egypt, the

Israelites were spared because of the blood that was applied to the doorposts of their homes. Christians have power over the enemy because of the blood of the New Covenant:

Behold, I give unto you power to tread on serpents and scorpions, and over all the power of the enemy: and nothing shall by any means hurt you (Luke 10:19).

There is something else that's really fascinating about these leucocytes. These white cells break down into four categories. Some of your white cells are short-timers; they live about 10 hours. But others live 60 to 70 years in your body. Some are called *antibodies*; they are for the body and against disease. When a disease attacks your body, an antibody that is familiar with that particular disease quickly multiplies itself and attacks the intruder.

For example, if you have had the measles, you won't get them again because there are antibodies in your system already familiar with that disease which were built up among your white cells the first time you got measles. So, if you are exposed to the measles, you don't have to worry about becoming infected again.

If you're exposed to something you're not immune to, like scarlet fever, your antibodies have never "met" scarlet fever before. The ones similar to the antibodies, which would normally fight scarlet fever, go to the rescue—but they can't totally conquer it. So scarlet fever enters the body. The antibodies will try different strategies against it; but by the time they find one that works, it's sometimes too late, and the person dies.

Sometimes, your body is unable to fight the disease, and doctors will try to find a vaccine. When you are vaccinated, you're inoculated with *"wise blood."* Wise blood contains antibodies taken from a person who has already had the disease. So when the disease comes knocking at your door, you already have an immunity to it even though you never had it before.

Jesus' blood fights sin in your life just like antibodies fight disease. Even though Jesus was tempted in every way you are, He never succumbed to sin. That makes His blood "wise blood." When you were born again, you were cleansed by His blood—inoculated with wise blood—so now you don't feel comfortable with sin and avoid sinful actions and situations. If you will allow Jesus' blood to work in you, it can make you completely immune to the temptations of sin (see Revelation 12:11).

Your Kinsman

Isn't it great to see all those wonderful benefits that are yours because of your Paternal inheritance? Because you have been born again by the blood of Jesus, when God looks at you, He looks at you through Jesus' blood. And so does the devil. He trembles because he knows you have power over him because of your Brother's blood line.

Did you know that you also have benefits because Jesus was *human* just like you? Jesus wasn't just the Son of God; He was also the **Son of man,** born of a virgin. In fact, Jesus referred to Himself more often as the "Son of man" than the "Son of God." It is the Son of man Who had no place to rest His head, the Son of man Who has power on the earth, the Son of man who suffered many things, the Son of man Who died on the Cross and rose from the dead; and it will be the Son of man Who comes in glory and Who sits on the right hand of the Father. So you see it is equally important to look at Jesus' human side as well as His divine side of the family.

Jesus became your "kin" through blood. He redeemed you not because you are good but because He is your kinsman-redeemer. When He shed His blood on the Cross, He redeemed you from your sins and ransomed your inheritance— not only an eternal inheritance as children of God, but all the earthly blessings God promised His children through the Old Testament blood covenants.

The Hebrew word *gaal* means "a next of kin who buys back a relative's property, marries his widow;" and "avenger, deliverer, ransomer, and

Release the Power of the Blood Covenant

redeemer." Leviticus 25:25 tells about a kinsman who redeems his brother's property:

If thy brother be waxen poor, and hath sold away some of his possession, and if any man of his kin come to redeem it, then shall he redeem that which his brother sold.

When a family member got into financial trouble, a relative could come to his rescue and redeem his property; in other words, get it out of hock. In this role, the kinsman redeemed his relative from a bad situation. The law of kinsman-redeemer didn't necessarily limit him to redeeming property, though. It could also pertain to a relative who sold himself as a slave as a last recourse:

And if a sojourner or stranger wax rich by thee, and thy brother that dwelleth by him wax poor, and sell himself unto the stranger or sojourner by thee, or to the stock of the stranger's family: After that he is sold he may be redeemed again; one of his brethren may redeem him: Either his uncle, or his uncle's son, may redeem him, or any that is nigh of kin unto him of his family may redeem him; or if he be able, he may redeem himself (Leviticus 25:47-49).

Here, the *gaal* is also a redeemer. Likewise, Jesus is your *gaal*, your kinsman-redeemer. He died to redeem you and restore to you all that sin had taken from you. He redeemed you from slavery to sin because you became His blood relative when you entered into covenant with God.

The first strong revelation of Jesus as our kinsman-redeemer is found in Job. Job was confident that someday he would see his redeemer stand upon the earth with his own eyes! He also knew his redeemer would be his kinsman, Who would ransom his body not just from slavery, not just from finances, but from death itself:

For I know that my redeemer liveth, and that he shall stand at the latter day upon the earth: And though after my skin worms destroy this body, yet in my flesh shall I see God: Whom I shall see for myself, and mine eyes shall behold, and not another; though my reins be consumed within me (Job 19:25,27).

That redeemer is Jesus—your blood brother and my blood brother. Even if worms destroy your body, someday you'll get a new body because of your kinsman-redeemer. Because of the blood of Jesus, Job and all believers will stand on this earth and see God.

A *gaal* could also secure a financial payment if his relative was murdered. The *gaal* could say, "You murdered my cousin; now sell your house and cattle, and give the money to my cousin's family to make up for what he would have provided for his family." In this role the kinsman stepped

Release the Power of the Blood Covenant

in to restore to the family their livelihood; the murderer would have to pay for his deed.

The role of the *gaal* also extended to marriage. The Levirate law said that the nearest kinsman had to marry the wife of a slain relative and raise up a child in the name of the deceased.

We see this beautifully portrayed in the book of Ruth. If you recall, Ruth was a Moabitess who married an Israelite when he and his family went to Moab to escape the famine in Bethlehem. After he died, Ruth and her mother-in-law, Naomi, returned to Bethlehem. There, Naomi prompted Ruth to go to Boaz, her kinsman, to "propose." Because her closest relative was unable to fulfill his *gaal* obligation, Boaz was able to step in as Ruth's *gaal*. Boaz was willing to marry Ruth and father a child in the name of his dead kin, but first he had to prove he was a relative. Then he had to put up the money to ransom (buy back) the land of her dead husband:

Moreover Ruth the Moabitess, the wife of Mahlon, have I purchased to be my wife, to raise up the name of the dead upon his inheritance, that the name of the dead be not cut off from among his brethren, and from the gate of his place: . . . So Boaz took Ruth, and she was his wife: and when he went in unto her, the LORD gave her conception, and she bare a son (Ruth 4:10,13).

Boaz is a picture of Jesus. Boaz fathered a child, Obed, but he could not claim him as his son; yet all three—Boaz, Ruth, and Obed are in Jesus' genealogy. Just as Boaz was the only one able to redeem Ruth from her situation, only Jesus could pay the price to ransom you from destruction. His blood—His sinless blood—alone could redeem you from sin. Jesus had to put up the price for you and me and it was expensive. Notice also, that we call Jesus "Savior" not "Father"; that's because He raised us up to be God's children, not His own, in a perfect picture of Levirate law.

As your *gaal*, Jesus is also your avenger. The blood of Jesus has no creed, race, or ethnic group. Ethiopia, Bosnia, Germany . . . all the hatred and killing result because people don't know a redeemer, a ransomer. They become their own *gaals*. If someone offends them, they have to avenge it. Yet God says, vengeance is His because He's our *gaal*. And just like in the Old Testament, where the kinsman-redeemer would go out and fight for his brothers, the kinsman-redeemer of the New Testament has already fought and won for His relatives—and that means YOU because you're in His blood line. Jesus will fight for you and cause you to win every time.

Jesus is your *gaal*. He is your redeemer, ransomer—"next of kin who buys back your property"—and your avenger, and deliverer.

Psalms 103:3,4 sums it up:

Who forgiveth all thine iniquities; who healeth all thy diseases; Who redeemeth thy life from destruction; who crowneth thee with lovingkindness and tender mercies.

All these benefits are yours because Jesus is your kinsman and you couldn't be kin without blood. The blood of Jesus gives you union with God. Because you have the blood, you can commune—become familiar—with God and know Him as "Abba Father." You have been adopted into the family of God:

For ye have not received the spirit of bondage again to fear; but ye have received the Spirit of adoption, whereby we cry, Abba, Father (Romans 8:15).

Finally, in the Old Testament, on the annual day of atonement, the high priest would go into the Holy of Holies and sprinkle blood on the mercy seat to make atonement for the sins of the people. You would think everybody would be gloomy, but it was never a down day because it was a day of new beginning. The day Jesus took His blood and put it on the Mercy Seat by the Father was the day of new beginning for mankind. Whoever receives the blood of Jesus has a new beginning, becomes a new creation, has a new Spirit, and gains a new life. Jesus makes all things new because He's your kinsman.

Chapter Six
Open-Heart Surgery

Do you realize that when you are born again, you have "open-heart" surgery? This is a *spiritual operation* that the Bible likens to the Jewish rite of circumcision—when God circumcises your heart, a covenant is established between you and God.

What does it mean to have a "circumcised heart"? If you recall, when we looked at the Abrahamic Covenant, God told Abraham to circumcise himself and all the males in his household as a sign of covenant relationship between God and himself. Abraham immediately obeyed God, thus establishing his seed forever:

This is my covenant, which ye shall keep, between me and you and thy seed after thee; Every man child among you shall be circumcised. And ye shall circumcise the flesh of your foreskin; and it shall be a token of the covenant betwixt me and you (Genesis 17:10-13).

Now the question arises, how do we get a circumcised heart? Circumcision of the heart is so important that God Himself performs the "operation":

> *In whom also ye are circumcised with the circumcision made without hands, in putting off the body of the sins of the flesh by the circumcision of Christ: . . . through the faith of the operation of God, . . .* (Colossians 2:11,12).

When you invite Jesus into your heart, He circumcises it. That means you have a scar on your heart that "marks" you as belonging to God. The Father, Son, and Holy Spirit are reminded of your covenant relationship each time they look at that scar. God also sets aside a robe of righteousness for you to wear; instead of your filthy robe, the new one is spotless because it comes through the blood of Jesus as a gift to you. You are robed in His righteousness because you bear the scar of heart circumcision. There are many more benefits that come from a circumcised heart. Let's look at them more closely.

Benefits of a Circumcised Heart

Before Joshua led the people to take Jericho, God told him to circumcise all the men who were born in the wilderness. These men had not been circumcised; so before they could enter the Promised Land, God required them to become a part of the covenant promises to Abraham. Joshua followed God's orders, circumcised them, and marked them for victory. And what happened?

Open-Heart Surgery

They marched around Jericho, shouted, the walls fell down, and the victory was theirs!

The circumcised heart marks you for victory too. God says, "I've marked you as a partaker of my covenant and that makes you more than a conqueror!" When your heart is circumcised, He that is in you is greater than he that is in the world and you stand victorious.

The mark of God also provides protection. Because Moses belonged to God, the baby Moses didn't sink when he floated down the Nile nor was he the appetizer for some hungry crocodile. Why? Because when Moses was circumcised, he was placed under God's protection. When Christ circumcises your heart, it's as if a hedge of protection is put up around you and nothing can hurt you (see Luke 10:19).

Let's look at what else circumcision produces. When Abraham received God's promise that he would be the father of a great nation, he was not circumcised. He and Sarah tried to produce an heir through their flesh nature. As a result, Ishmael was born. It was not until *after* Abraham was circumcised—when he was about 100 years old— that God gave him Isaac. Ishmael was born out of the flesh nature, but Isaac was born out of his spirit nature. The "Isaacs" of your life will only be born after your heart is circumcised.

How many times have you heard someone say,

"I wish I could start my life all over again"? I think most people have felt this way at least once in their lives. God can circumcise your heart, give you a new nature, and open your heart to the things of God. When your heart is circumcised, you are given a new beginning! Your new life begins with a new name: you are called a Christian and you are included in the Lamb's Book of Life!

Circumcision of the heart refers to cutting off the lust and passion of the flesh so you can hear from God and His new nature can come into you. Your old, flesh nature can only produce "Ishmaels." But your new nature produces new beginnings! When you enter into blood covenant with God, He opens your heart to the things of the Lord, and nothing is impossible through Jesus.

Here's some more good news: Jesus can handle the "impossible" people in your life. We are all going to meet some people who look pretty rough sometimes, but that doesn't mean that Jesus can't mark their hearts and get through to them.

Now what do you suppose happens if you choose not to have this "elective surgery"? God told Abraham that if any man was not circumcised, he would be cut off from God because he had broken His covenant (see Genesis 17:14). That man would be punished, even to the point of death, if he was not circumcised. In fact, Moses' son almost died because he wasn't circumcised

Open-Heart Surgery

(see Exodus 4:24-26).

God wants you to serve Him; however, no man can serve God in the flesh. If you were to say, "I love God, I was born into a Christian home, I have a heart for God, and I'm going to serve Him"—but you're not born again—then you are producing works of the flesh, which profit nothing (see John 6:63). The works of the flesh do not produce the work of God; however, a circumcised heart gives you a new nature with which to serve God.

A circumcised heart opens you up to the things of God, brings about your new nature, protects you, and marks you for victory rather than defeat. Are you walking in defeat? Are you living in the flesh? Do you desire to change your life, hear from God, and start walking in victory, protection, and a new way of life? Then tell God you want to have "open-heart surgery," and let Him cut His covenant with you!

Chapter Seven
The Blood and the Word

The blood and the Word go together. When God gave His Word to Moses, He told him to sprinkle it with blood. The blood reconciles people to God based upon His Word in Leviticus 17:11. All the benefits, terms, and blessings of your blood covenant with God are detailed in the Bible—the Word of God—beginning in the Old Testament and ending in Revelation. The Word also binds God to His people by His oath (Hebrews 6:17,18). So it is that the blood and the Word are the two components of your covenant with God: you must have both to overcome Satan!

Revelation 12:11 declares that believers overcome Satan by *". . . the **blood** of the Lamb, and by the **word** of their testimony; . . . ."* From the time God killed an animal to provide a covering for Adam and Eve, to the saints' victory over Satan, the blood and the Word work powerfully on man's behalf.

You've already seen that Jesus' blood gives you certain privileges and a definite inheritance, but without God's Word how would you know what those are? In order to claim those promises, you

Release the Power of the Blood Covenant

first have to know what the Word says about them. Then you can claim them for your family as well. When God told Abraham He would make a covenant with him, He told Abraham to circumcise his sons; they in turn were to circumcise their sons. Why? Because God's intention was for the covenant to continue throughout all generations, and His intentions still stand for you and your family today. Jesus' blood and Word are for you, your descendants, and your loved ones.

I know a woman who applied Jesus' blood and God's Word to her unsaved husband and after many years, saw him saved. Though both Billie and her husband had been raised in Christian homes, she realized he did not have the same "call of God" on his life that she had. When they dated, Art accompanied her to church, but after they married, he only went with her on special occasions. Nevertheless, he encouraged her to serve the Lord.

After 15 years of marriage, God began to open doors of ministry for Billie. She started teaching Bible studies, then eventually traveled with me, leading worship and special music. Art continued to encourage Billie, and eventually she went into full-time ministry. It was during that time that a friend gave her a set of tapes about the power of the blood. When she listened to them, she realized the importance of the blood and the Word working together.

She combined the blood with three simple scriptures: according to II Corinthians 4:3,4, she began to pray that the blindness be removed from Art's eyes; that laborers be sent to him (Matthew 9:38); and that Art's heart be washed in the blood of Jesus, according to Hebrews 9:13,14.

Though Billie had asked for laborers before, she never realized that a "spiritually blind" person can't see or hear the laborers; so she prayed Ephesians 1:17,18 several times a day to ready him for the laborers. As Christmas approached, the Holy Spirit impressed upon her to ask Art to read through the Bible as a family. A few months later, they began praying together before Art left for work, praying to be washed in the blood of Jesus and made one in Spirit.

Little by little Billie saw her husband transformed before her eyes. The next Christmas, Art told Billie his Christmas gift to her was that he was going to church with her. She thought he meant for just that one service, but the next Sunday he attended church with her and was baptized in water and in the Spirit. Earlier, Art had given his heart to Jesus watching Christian television.

Billie AND Art work together now in full-time ministry. God made them one mind, one spirit, and even perfected their one-flesh relationship. ***That's because there is power in the blood of Jesus!***

Upon the shed blood of Jesus rests every facet of your covenant with God. Every promise, every provision in God's Word, is yours through the blood of Jesus. Yet so many Christians have claimed only the cleansing from sin and missed the rest of what God has provided.

The Old Testament covenants foreshadowed a great many of God's provisions for you today. In addition, the promises of the New Covenant guarantee you, as citizens of the kingdom of God, certain blessings, rights, and freedoms. So let's look at some of them so you can see exactly what you are entitled to as a child of God.

Multiplied Blessings

The Bible says that believers can claim all the blessings that pertain to the righteous. In fact, one of your blessings *is **righteousness*** which comes with forgiveness and eternal life:

But of him are ye in Christ Jesus, who of God is made unto us wisdom, and righteousness, and sanctification, and redemption (I Corinthians 1:30).

Righteousness makes you "sin-conscious." Not only is your conscience made acutely aware of sin in your life, you are also extremely conscious of

The Blood and the Word

your remedy for sin—the blood of Jesus. Furthermore, righteousness makes you fearless in Satan's presence.

One of the most precious blessings is that you are **united with God** through the blood of Christ; you are grafted into the vine (Jesus). That means you can also produce the same fruit that He does, and you have the same life as Jesus because your life comes from Him.

Those in covenant with God also have a **revelation of God**. This revelation comes through studying the life of Jesus and through the Holy Spirit. You can know His works and His ways; but most importantly, you can know Him. Jesus tells you everything He learns from the Father giving you a revelation of God. As a covenant partner, you can become so intimately acquainted with God, that you are also called His "friend":

Henceforth I call you not servants; for the servant knoweth not what his lord doeth: but I have called you friends; for all that I have heard of my Father I have made known unto you (John 15:15).

You are also blessed with **victory over your enemies**. Jesus' supremacy over everything means that He has disarmed every power and authority that comes against you—He triumphed over them at the Cross. Your enemies were defeated almost 2,000 years ago—fear, discouragement, financial problems, generation curses, have all been conquered on the Cross:

> *Blotting out the handwriting of ordinances that was against us, which was contrary to us, and took it out of the way, nailing it to his cross; And having spoiled principalities and powers, he made a shew of them openly, triumphing over them in it* (Colossians 2:14,15).

When you claim the blood, you gain ***power and authority over the power of Satan and his demons*** (see Luke 10:19). Your might and strength have nothing to do with your size, poise, training, or physical strength. Your victory comes from the authority you were given and the power you possess through the blood of Jesus Christ.

Part of that power and authority comes because you have ***the name of Jesus***. What a blessing! The name of Jesus will always bear fruit for it is the name above all names. In the name of Jesus you can do all things. John 16:23,24 tells us that the Father will give you whatever you ask when you use the name of Jesus. So whatever needs you have—healing, finances, restoration of relationships—claim them in the name of Jesus and put the devil to flight!

In fact, the New Covenant frees you from worrying about your needs. You have an abundant supply, and ***all your needs are met*** through Christ Jesus (see Philippians 4:19). Because the earth and fullness thereof is the Lord's, you can lay claim to its fullness as His rightful heir.

Through the New Covenant, you are blessed with the *same anointing that was upon Jesus*. Jesus had an anointing in His spirit, soul, and body. The anointing in His spirit allowed Him to understand the spirits of others. The anointing in His soul gave Him an overwhelming compassion for people—Scripture tells us He was often so moved, He wept. The anointing on His body was so strong that it strengthened Him and gave Him the ability to face the Cross. Likewise, Jesus' anointing will affect your whole life. You can use Jesus' anointing to understand what your children are going through. Apply Jesus' anointing to your own soul the next time you see a homeless person on the streets of your town. And the next time you are faced with a crisis, apply His anointing for a favorable outcome.

The New Covenant Bill of Rights

Just as the Bill of Rights gives Americans certain inalienable rights, the Bible guarantees Christians certain rights and privileges that are irrevocable and everlasting.

The New Covenant guarantees that you have the *right of counsel and provides you with a defense attorney*, an advocate with the Father. Because Jesus always was and always will be, He will always be available to defend you. You don't

Release the Power of the Blood Covenant

have to depend on your own defense, even when the devil tries to pull a "fast one" on your Defender. Jesus has heard all the accusations before; He has defended Christians against everything the devil could ever come up with. And Jesus has never lost a case! Furthermore, Jesus is always working on your behalf, yet He never sends you a bill—though His work is not cheap, it is free.

Because Jesus lives inside you, He knows all the intricacies of your case so no one can bring a surprise witness against you. God doesn't expect you to sin, but if you do, Christ will defend you:

. . . And if any man sin, we have an advocate with the Father, Jesus Christ the righteous: And he is the propitiation for our sins: and not for our's only, but also for the sins of the whole world (I John 2:1,2).

Even with all the benefits you have because Jesus is your Advocate, an added advantage to every Christian is the fact that Jesus Christ is equal with God and equal with man. Lawyers are not on an equal basis with the judge because the court system puts the judge above the attorney. Jesus knows how to represent God because He is God; and He knows how to represent man because He is man. Furthermore, He serves in the highest court of the universe:

Now of the things which we have spoken this is the sum: We have such an high priest, who is set on the right hand of the throne of the Majesty in the heavens (Hebrews 8:1).

You have a ***threefold right to life*** because there was a threefold curse of death on you which was removed when you accepted Christ as your Lord and Savior. When Adam sinned, he died spiritually; he was no longer in communion with God. Sin separated him from God and that separation brought spiritual death. The whole human race experiences spiritual death because of Adam's sin: *"For as in Adam all die, even so in Christ shall all be made alive"* (I Corinthians 15:22).

Without Jesus, death reigns in your emotions, intellect, and will. But with Jesus, all that changes. The New Covenant guarantees you spiritual life, strengthens your inner man (soul), and quickens your mortal body. You pass from death into life. God wants you to have life in your inner man. He wants your mind to be so renewed by the Word that you continually obey the Holy Spirit. The Word renews your soul and brings new life to your emotions, intellect, and will. You have a right to life in your mortal body. God promises that He will quicken your mortal body through His Spirit:

But if the Spirit of him that raised up Jesus from the dead dwell in you, he that raised up Christ from the dead shall also quicken your mortal bodies by His Spirit that dwelleth in you (Romans 8:11).

You have a full provision for health and healing through the New Covenant, which guarantees you the *right to health*. God repeatedly tells you in His Word that Jesus died not just for your spiritual health but also for your physical health—so you know He must mean it! In fact, you know that healing is an integral benefit of the New Covenant when you look at Jesus' earthly ministry:

When the even was come, they brought unto him many that were possessed with devils: and he cast out the spirits with his word, and healed all that were sick: That it might be fulfilled which was spoken by Esaias the prophet, saying, Himself took our infirmities, and bare our sicknesses (Matthew 8:16,17).

Healing is in the atonement. From the Old Testament, you learn that the curse included all manner of diseases (see Deuteronomy 28:16-52). Jesus was made a curse for you, and at the same time, redeemed you from the curse of the law (see Galatians 3:13). First Peter 2:24 says that Jesus bore your sicknesses and diseases in His body on the Cross, and by His stripes, you **have been healed.**

Plead the Blood

Now that you know what the New Covenant offers every believer through the blood of Jesus,

The Blood and the Word

it's time for you to **release the power of the blood covenant!** In other words, start putting faith into action and begin claiming your rights, privileges, and blessings by pleading the blood of Jesus. Now, let me guess. You're probably saying, "But, Marilyn, how do I do that?"

In order to plead the blood of Jesus and do it correctly, you need to draw near to God and have your heart sprinkled. Just like the priests in the Old Testament who continually sprinkled the blood of the sacrificed animals for the sins of the people, you need to keep coming to the altar—to the Mercy Seat—to have your heart sprinkled with the blood of Jesus. This is accomplished through prayer. Prayer is your hot line to God, and the Cross is the fiber-optic cable. Faster than a blink of an eye, God hears you:

Call unto me, and I will answer thee, and shew thee great and mighty things, which thou knowest not (Jeremiah 33:3).

You must also maintain communication with God. Keep a clear conscience and live obediently to the Word. You must live on "unleavened bread." In other words, when you sin, receive forgiveness and remain clean of sin. (The devil can use sin in your life to take your confidence away.)

It is also imperative that you recognize that you have been bought with a price—Jesus' blood. His blood keeps you safe from the dangers that

Release the Power of the Blood Covenant

abound in this world. Jesus' blood is so priceless that, you who have been purchased with it, are of great value to the Father. No one else in the universe has the right to you because you have been bought with a price. So when you plead the blood of Jesus, heaven pays attention because the blood was very expensive.

You can use the blood of Jesus against the enemy. When the devil is at work in your life, apply the blood to the situation by faith and by speaking the Word. Have faith in what the blood of Jesus has done for you. Take the authority that was given you through the New Covenant and immobilize the enemy.

Demons can't stand it when you plead the blood of Jesus because His blood is the symbol of their total defeat. Jesus triumphed over the works of the enemy through His blood on the Cross. So, whenever you're coming against the enemy, use the word, "blood"; it makes hell shudder!

You have the name of Jesus compounded with His blood—and there isn't a more powerful weapon. With your words you can wield the greatest weapon the world will ever know! So when the devil comes against you, say, "In the name of Jesus, you leave!" But if you want to be stronger you can add, "Because of the covenant I have with Jesus and because of the blood that was shed on Calvary, you MUST leave!"

The Blood and the Word

Once he has fled, fill the empty places with the Spirit of God. Don't give the devil an inch of your territory. If he thinks he can gain an entrance back into your life, he will surely take advantage of the situation. But if you're covered from head to toe in the blood of Jesus, if you plead the blood over all your loved ones, and if you keep that blood as a shield around your home, car, office, and neighborhood, the devil can't get to you. Ask the Holy Spirit to reveal to you any weak spots in your defenses. He'll show you areas in your life that you may not have turned over to God yet, and then He'll teach you how to surrender them to God rather than the devil.

From the moment you accept Jesus Christ as your Savior and Lord, the power of the New Covenant is yours. You can now walk in victory every day of your life because you have the authority, Word, blood, and the name of Jesus Christ to wield as your weapons against Satan.

The blood of the New Covenant also prevents you from becoming complacent. Just because you know you're going to heaven, doesn't mean you can become oblivious to those around you who are going to hell. The blood gives you the compassion you need to go out and win unbelievers to Christ, and the boldness to proclaim His Word to the world.

Even after you die, the blood will continue to

Release the Power of the Blood Covenant

work for you. One day you will stand at the Judgment Seat of Christ, your Advocate and Defender. God will look at the book that records all your sins, but He won't be able to see them because they're covered with red—the blood of Jesus. Then He'll open the book of works. There He will see that while you were on earth, you led a woman to the Lord who brought her children to church where they got saved. But that's not all! One of those children became a missionary and ended up leading a whole village to the Lord! All those people are credited to your account! Oh, what a day of rejoicing it will be when—because of the blood of Jesus—you finally hear:

*... Well done, thou good and faithful servant: thou hast been faithful over a few things, I will make thee ruler over many things: **enter thou into the joy of thy lord*** (Matthew 25:21).

I'll see you there!

Receive Jesus Christ as Lord and Savior of Your Life.

The Bible says, *"That if thou shalt confess with thy mouth the Lord Jesus, and shalt believe in thine heart that God hath raised him from the dead, thou shalt be saved. For with the heart man believeth unto righteousness; and with the mouth confession is made unto salvation"* (Romans 10:9,10).

To receive Jesus Christ as Lord and Savior of your life, sincerely pray this prayer from your heart:

Dear Jesus,

I believe that You died for me and that You rose again on the third day. I confess to You that I am a sinner and that I need Your love and forgiveness. Come into my life, forgive my sins, and give me eternal life. I confess You now as my Lord. Thank You for my salvation!

Signed _____

Date _____

Write to us.
We will send you information to help you with your new life in Christ.

Marilyn Hickey Ministries • P.O. Box 17340
Denver, CO 80217 • (303) 770-0400

BOOKS BY MARILYN HICKEY

A Cry for Miracles ($5.95)
Acts of the Holy Spirit ($7.95)
Angels All Around ($7.95)
Armageddon ($3.95)
Ask Marilyn ($8.95)
Be Healed ($8.95)
The Bible Can Change You ($12.95)
The Book of Revelation Comic Book ($3.00)
Break the Generation Curse ($7.95)
Daily Devotional ($5.95)
Dear Marilyn ($5.95)
Divorce Is Not the Answer ($4.95)
Especially for Today's Woman ($14.95)
Freedom From Bondages ($4.95)
Gift Wrapped Fruit ($2.00)
God's Covenant for Your Family ($5.95)
God's Rx for a Hurting Heart ($3.50)
How To Be a Mature Christian ($5.95)
Know Your Ministry ($3.50)
Maximize Your Day . . . God's Way ($7.95)
Release the Power of the Blood Covenant ($3.95)
The Names of God ($7.95)
The No. 1 Key to Success—Meditation ($3.50)
Satan-Proof Your Home ($7.95)
Save the Family Promise Book ($14.95)
Signs in the Heavens ($5.95)
What Every Person Wants to Know About Prayer ($3.95)
When Only a Miracle Will Do ($3.95)
Your Miracle Source ($3.50)
Your Personality Workout ($5.95)
Your Total Health Handbook—Body • Soul • Spirit ($9.95)

MINI-BOOKS: 75¢ each
by Marilyn Hickey

Beat Tension
Bold Men Win
Bulldog Faith
Change Your Life
Children Who Hit the Mark
Conquering Setbacks
Experience Long Life
Fasting and Prayer
God's Benefit: Healing
God's Seven Keys to Make You Rich
Hold On to Your Dream
How To Become More Than a Conqueror
How To Win Friends
I Can Be Born Again and Spirit Filled
I Can Dare To Be an Achiever
Keys to Healing Rejection
The Power of Forgiveness
The Power of the Blood
Receiving Resurrection Power
Renew Your Mind
Solving Life's Problems
Speak the Word
Standing in the Gap
The Story of Esther
Tithes • Offerings • Alms • God's Plan for Blessing You
Winning Over Weight
Women of the Word